ILLUSTRATED TALES OF
SURREY

EDDY GREENFIELD

AMBERLEY

Acknowledgements

At the time of writing, Covid-19 is still with us and travelling to get the required illustrations for this book in person simply hasn't been possible. I wish to give my most grateful acknowledgements to all those making available the public domain and Creative Commons images used in this book.

First published 2022

Amberley Publishing
The Hill, Stroud
Gloucestershire, GL5 4EP

www.amberley-books.com

British Library Cataloguing in Publication Data.
A catalogue record for this book is available from the British Library.

ISBN 978 1 3981 1112 7 (paperback)
ISBN 978 1 3981 1113 4 (ebook)

Origination by Amberley Publishing.
Printed in Great Britain.

Contents

Introduction

'The men of Surrey, Checky Blew and gold,
(Which for brave Warren their first Earle they wore,
In many a Field that honour'd was of olde)'.
The Battaile of Agincourt, Michael Drayton, 1627

When even the county's flag is immortalised in a poem by one of the Elizabethan Age's most respected bards, it is not surprising that Surrey – despite being one of the smallest of the English counties – is home to many traditions, stories, myths and legends.

This book will explore many of these stories that have grown up around the Surrey landscape – some founded in fact, others less so – from the origin myths of various geographic features to famous legendary personalities, strange mysteries, and peculiar histories, from stories that have passed down through the generations to more recent urban legends.

So, strap in tight. We're about to go on a magical mystery tour into the strange world where things really do go bump in the night, where dark shapes linger in the shadows, and there is that uncanny feeling that you are not alone. We are going to venture into that mystical twilight zone where historical fact and fantastic fiction merge, and where nothing is ever quite as it seems.

I think the first stop on our journey is fast approaching. In fact, it may be as near as turning the next page. Will you join me?

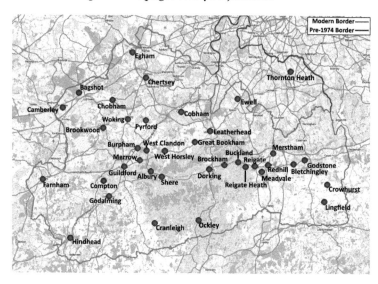

Map of Surrey. (Open-StreetMap)

Cocker Nash

Our journey begins in the far west of Surrey, in the historic town of Farnham. The tale of The Old Drunk is one that pervades almost every region, and Surrey's own version is that of an old fish hawker by the name of Cocker Nash (pronounced 'Naish' in the Surrey dialect). The story goes that Nash decided to spend his day's takings in the pub drinking to warm his bones after a busy day peddling through the winter streets. By nightfall, and after having his fill, Cocker made his way home. However, he soon became lost in the woods at Waverley. As any sensible person ought to do when lost and frightened, he called out: 'Man lost! Man lost!'

He waited. A distant retort was heard – an answer perhaps?

He cried out again: 'Man lost! Man lost!'

Again came the reply: 'Who? Who?'

Frantic now, he screamed at the top of his voice, 'Cocker Nash, of Farnham'.

Unfortunately, the only response Cocker ever got was the same, for it was not a would-be rescuer that wanted to know who he was, but a pigeon going 'coo, coo'.

Woodland, near Waverley, where Cocker Nash became lost. (Don Cload)

The Hare and the Herring

Farnham can also lay claim to Cocker Nash's antithesis, since the town's famous son, William Cobbett, once used his wit to trick some hunters and save the life of an innocent hare. Writing in an 1807 edition of his weekly political newspaper, Cobbett related the story of how, when he was a boy living in Farnham, he used to tie a smelly red herring to a piece of string and drag it 'four or five miles over hedges and ditches, across fields and through coppices' in order to lure the hunters' hounds well away from the fields where he saw the hares having a merry time and ensure that none of the long-eared creatures would come to harm.

There is some doubt, however, as to whether Cobbett really carried out such acts, since the purpose of his retelling of this story was merely as a prologue to a political attack on some of his opponents, who he believed were misleading the public with their own 'red herrings'.

William Cobbett's birthplace. (Julian Osley)

The appropriately named Fox Way on Cobbett Hill, Farnham. (James Emmans)

William Cobbett's grave, Farnham. (Jack1956)

Mother Ludlam

A narrow woodland path on the way towards Waverley Abbey is perhaps not the place one would expect to find a story of white witches and fairies, nor is Frensham Church the obvious place to come across a witch's cauldron. However, if you were to take the Moor Park footpath alongside the River Wey, you will come across the entrance to a large cave; and, indeed, a large copper cauldron, about 3 feet in diameter and half as deep, does sit within St Mary's Church at Frensham.

The earliest known mention of the legend is in John Aubrey's 1673 travelogue, *The Natural History and Antiquities of Surrey*, in which he speaks of the cauldron having been 'brought hither by the fairies … from Borough-hill, about a mile hence'. Although not mentioning a witch or Mother Ludlam by name, he went on to describe the ritual that people carried out in relation to the later legends that brought in those elements. 'There is a cave,' he says, 'where some have fancied to hear music'. Within this cave was a great stone, measuring about 6 feet long, upon which the petitioner would rap their knuckles and declare what they desired to borrow, and when they would repay (or return) the item. A mysterious voice would answer when the petitioner should return, and upon doing so the petitioner would find their desired item waiting for them upon the stone. Aubrey's tale states that the cauldron was one such item borrowed in this manner, but was not returned to the cave on time and thus broke the spell, 'and ever since that time no borrowing there'.

Over the centuries the legend has been altered, embellished and adapted to include different elements; for example, the cauldron is sometimes said to have

Mother Ludlam's Cave.
(Andrew Bowden)

been used by Mother Ludlam to make her potions. Another variation places the magic stone at the Devil's Jumps rather than at the cave. A mid-twentieth-century adaptation adds in the devil, and claims that it was he who approached the cave and asked to borrow Mother Ludlam's cauldron. However, observing the tell-tale hoofprints in the sand, the request was refused and so the devil stole the vessel instead. She gave chase and the two of them bounded across the countryside, and wherever the devil's feet touched the earth, hills sprouted out of the ground to create the Devil's Jumps at nearby Churt. On the last of these hills he dropped the cauldron, and Mother Ludlam took it to Frensham church for safe keeping.

Additionally, a second, smaller cave is found above Mother Ludlam's Cave, and it has developed its own mythology of a gentleman from London named Foote, who was (as labelled at the time) a 'lunatic'. Having travelled down to Farnham with a large travel case, he hired a man to take the case to the gate of Moor Park. Foote fell suddenly ill and entered the cave. From here, he (and his case) was taken to the local workhouse infirmary. Here, the case was opened and the porters found that it was full of old buttons. With his dying breath, Foote exclaimed 'It's gold! Gold!'

Above left: Mother Ludlam's Cauldron in Frensham Church. (BabelStone)

Above right: Father Foote's Cave. (Andrew West)

St Dunstan's Tongs

Although now only fragmentary ruins, Waverley Abbey was once a significant site of religious worship in Surrey and once contained wall paintings of St Dunstan and the devil.

It is said that while he was in holy orders at Glastonbury, St Dunstan met the devil. Old Nick tried his best to tempt St Dunstan away from his good work, pestering and pestering him. St Dunstan did his best to ignore and turn a blind eye, until he could take no more; picking up a pair of tongs, he pinched the devil by the nose and squeezed it so hard that the devil let out a scream that could be heard 3 miles away.

The devil did not give up on his task and later returned disguised as a traveller whose horse needed re-shoeing. St Dunstan agreed, but saw that something was not quite right. Seeing that the horse was really the devil in disguise, he nailed the shoe into the latter's foot. The devil let out great shrieks of pain and begged St Dunstan to remove the nails. He agreed to do so on condition that the devil never set foot in any house marked with a horseshoe, thereby giving rise (it is said) to the custom of hanging a horseshoe on one's door for luck.

All traces of St Dunstan at Waverley have long since vanished, as has much of the abbey itself. However, his name, and legend, lives on in Surrey, with a statue of him (with his devil-tongs in hand) within St Dunstan's Church in Woking.

Above left: Ruins of Waverley Abbey. (Colin Smith)

Above right: The refectory ruins, Waverley. (Bill Nicholls)

The Camberley Obelisk

Sitting atop a wooded hill behind Langley Drive in Camberley are the remains of a red-brick tower standing just over 9 metres tall. In its heyday – sometime between 1765 and 1770 – it would have reached up to 30 metres in height and was topped with crenulations; each face of the tower contained a large window on each floor and almost resembled a church tower.

The structure was built by John Norris, a minor nobleman of the mid to late eighteenth century. Its purpose is shrouded in mystery; various theories suggest it was a viewing platform, an inland lighthouse for people on the heath, a watchtower, or simply a nobleman's folly.

However, the story takes an interesting turn when delving deeper into John Norris' background. He was a close friend of Sir Francis Dashwood, who made his home at West Wycombe, Berkshire, approximately 21 miles north of Camberley. Norris also had a second home at West Wycombe, and the men were members of the infamous Hellfire Club set up by Dashwood in caves on his estate.

The Camberley Obelisk ruins.
(Len Williams)

Shortly before Norris built his tower at Camberley, Dashwood had a large, hollow wooden ball – covered entirely in gold leaf – erected atop the tower of St Lawrence's Church at West Wycombe. Inside were wooden benches to accommodate several people, and a small porthole on the south side (facing towards Camberley) was the only window looking out.

It has been suggested that the two men used their towers to communicate secret messages to each other using heliographs (flashes of sunlight). The Hellfire Club was strict on secrecy, and so any written correspondence would have been kept to a minimum; such a means of communication would not be an unreasonable assumption.

However, the story takes another turn in the late 1770s, when the American War of Independence was in full swing. It was in his role as Postmaster General that Dashwood was in a position to intercept communications from the revolutionary colonial forces, which he passed onto the British spymaster, Lord Auckland. It has been suggested that Norris was recruited as one of Dashwood's agents, since a cryptic line in a letter from Norris, dated 3 June 1778, states 'Did this day Heliograph Intelligence from Dr Franklin in Paris to Wycombe'. Stranger still is the fact that Dr Franklin was none other than Benjamin Franklin, and it would appear that while Dashwood was feeding intelligence against the revolutionaries to the British state, Norris was acting as a go between to pass secret messages between Franklin in Paris and Dashwood in Berkshire.

Was Franklin secretly working as a British agent? Unlikely. Were Dashwood and Norris secretly working as double agents for the colonialists? Unlikely. Were Franklin and Dashwood simply trying to maintain their close friendship despite officially being bitter enemies? Possibly. The whole affair surrounding the Camberley Obelisk, and any potential involvement in the American Revolutionary War, throws up more mysteries and questions than it solves – as all good folklore should.

Dashwood's golden ball at West Wycombe church. (Pickled Egg)

The Golden Farmer

Around a century before Norris built his strange tower in the modern-day centre of Camberley, the heath that once covered this area was a key highway for stagecoaches between London and the south coast, with as many as thirty coaches a day passing through. Naturally such a bounty of riches would also attract another sort of person: the highwayman. Even Dick Turpin himself is reputed to have used the King's Arms in Bagshot and the nearby Golden Farmer pub.

However, it is not Dick Turpin to which this story pertains, but the Golden Farmer for whom the pub was named. This man was called William Davies, a Welshman by birth, but who lived at Sodbury in Gloucestershire with his wife and eighteen children. From here, the family moved to Frimley in Surrey in the mid-1640s. With such a large family to feed, it is not surprising that this farmer turned his eyes to more profitable endeavours. Davies' favourite haunt was Bagshot Heath, but he had a more expensive taste than your average highwayman. As his nickname suggests, our Golden Farmer would accept nothing less than gold.

It would appear that no one ever suspected this wealthy farmer despite having the reputation of paying his way in gold coins. Or, perhaps, no one bothered to ask, because some of the liberated gold often found itself being pushed under the doors of the local poor families by their very own Robin Hood. Davies perfected his night-time trade and plied it with expertise that few other highwaymen ever did. Becoming a complete master of disguise, Davies' victims included the Duchess of Albemarle, Sir Thomas Day, and even his own landlord.

Davies became wealthy enough that he was able to retire from robbing coaches for some years, although the attraction of gold causes men to do strange things, and in 1690, aged sixty-four, the urge to return to his youthful ways was too strong. Teaming up with his old accomplice, Thomas Sympson (alias Old Mobb), and having lost some of his former expertise he was recognised during a job. Fleeing to Westminster, he was spotted and pursued through the streets, shooting a butcher in order to make his escape. This was a desperate act; until now Davies had been able to rely upon his charm rather than force to get his victims to hand over their worldly goods.

Now wanted for murder as well as highway robbery, the Golden Farmer of Frimley was a marked man. He was soon arrested, convicted, and hanged in December 1690, although not before leaving clues as to the identity of Old Mobbs, who Davies believed had betrayed him. Davies' body was then brought to Bagshot Heath to hang in chains on the gibbet close to the site of the former Golden Farmer pub. Old Mobbs met with a similar fate the following year.

The Golden Farmer pub was later renamed the Jolly Farmer, and retained the name when a modern replacement was built on the same site. The pub is now closed, but the legend of Surrey's own Robin Hood lives on.

Former Jolly Farmer pub near Bagshot. (Alan Hunt)

Gibbet Hill and the Unknown Sailor

The highest point of the scarp surrounding the Devil's Punch Bowl at Hindhead has the rather unpleasant name of Gibbet Hill. However, it is not a gibbet that you will find here, but a large Celtic Cross marking the scene of a grisly murder that occurred here on 24 September 1786. The victim's name has never been recorded, and he is referred to simply as the Unknown Sailor.

The Sailor had stopped for refreshments at the Red Lion in Thursley on his way to Portsmouth, and met three other sailors in the pub. He seemed to have struck up a rapport with these men and purchased drinks for all of them before continuing on his journey south. The men followed the Sailor and as they got to the isolated spot of Gibbet Hill, they murdered him and robbed his body of his clothes and possessions.

The men were soon apprehended at the Sun Inn in Rake a few hours later as they tried to sell the Sailor's clothes, and taken to Kingston to await trial. On 7 April 1787, the three men were executed for their crime; as was the custom of the time, their bodies were then brought back to the scene of the crime and hanged in the gibbet. The bodies were still present on 23 December 1790, when lightning struck and knocked one of the corpses to the ground.

The murder so shocked the locals for years to come that the villagers of Thursley paid for the Sailor to be buried with full dignity in St Michael and All Angel's churchyard, and for a headstone to be erected at his grave (which has recently been Grade I listed).

Another memorial stone was erected close to the scene of the murder. The stone was moved and re-moved several times between 1826 and 1932 despite the following warning being engraved on the back of the stone in 1827:

Cursed be the Man who injureth
or removeth this Stone

Finally, the Celtic Cross was erected by Sir William Erle in 1851 to mark the site of the gibbet and to seemingly try and draw a line under the incident after almost a century. Nonetheless, the event and the various memorials still fascinate and draw stories. Even as recently as 1984 it was reported that a mysterious stranger left flowers at the grave on each anniversary, and that several of those responsible for moving the memorial stone atop Gibbet Hill have met with unfortunate ends.

The Unknown Sailor's grave at Thursley. (BTP51)

Watts Chapel

The Watts Cemetery chapel is a sight to behold. This red-brick chapel was the brainchild of the Compton artist Mary Fraser-Tytler, wife of the famed Victorian painter and sculptor George Frederic Watts, when a new burial ground was opened in the village. Mary did not just want to have a chapel erected, but to get the whole community involved, particularly among the poorer members of the village. Almost every villager became involved in building the chapel between 1896 and 1898, laying the bricks, sculpting the hundreds of terracotta tiles that decorate the structure, or decorating the interior with Celtic-Christian imagery, frescoes and paintings. Once the building was completed, it formed the shape of a cross centred on a round room that curved upwards into the apex.

The chapel is open to visits every day, free of charge, and is well worth a trip. The cemetery also contains the grave of Aldous Huxley, as well as memorials to Mary and her husband.

Above left: Watt's Cemetery Chapel. (Stefan Czapski)

Above right: Detail of the chapel decoration. (Alan Hunt)

A Railway for the Dead

You know you are delving into something a bit spooky and unsettling when the company involved is named the London Necropolis Company and its logo features a skull and crossbones, the sands of time and a snake eating its own tail. Yet, it took such a company to create a solution to the crisis facing London in the mid-nineteenth century. The capital's graveyards and cemeteries were full to bursting point; after periods of heavy rain coffins and corpses were floating up to the surface. All the cemeteries were closed by an Act of Parliament and 2,000 acres of ground at Brookwood was secured to create what was then the world's largest cemetery – a city for the dead.

Like all good cities, a railway service was essential to serve its 'inhabitants'. Fortunately, the site chosen for Brookwood Cemetery sat adjacent to the main London & South West Railway line, and so it was a case of building a private sideline off the main tracks through the cemetery. A pair of railway stations was also built within the cemetery. The first funeral train departed London's Waterloo Station in November 1854, carrying the bodies of stillborn twins to their resting place at Brookwood.

The railway continued in operation until the last train arrived in 1941. It closed down for the remainder of the war years, and afterwards it was decided that it was too expensive to reinstate service. The railway infrastructure was removed from Brookwood in 1976, although traces of it still survive.

Above left: A section of the Railway of the Dead, Brookwood. (Bill Nicholls)

Above right: Former cemetery railway platform. (Mary Percy)

The Rabbit Woman

Mary Toft was born in Godalming in around 1701. Her early life is unrecorded, and may have passed entirely without record if it weren't for her story of the rabbits.

When Mary fell pregnant in 1726, she miscarried after apparently becoming spellbound by a rabbit seen bounding about the place. A few days later she gave birth to a creature resembling a half-formed rabbit. Guildford surgeon John Howard was called upon to attend to Mary despite his scepticism as to her story. About a fortnight later, the surgeon was called upon again by Mary after having given birth to several more rabbits. All in all, Mary claimed to have delivered nine rabbits (all dead), as well as various other animal parts, including three legs of a tabby cat, a rabbit leg, and part of an eel.

Mary told the flabbergasted surgeon that about two months previously she had seen a rabbit while working out in the fields, and gave chase. She became so enamoured with the animal that she miscarried her child and fell ill, since which time she was unable to stop thinking about rabbits.

Mary Toft. (Wellcome Collection)

The story spread far and wide, with some considering it a miracle 'fit to be presented to the Royal Society,' and others considering it an aberration of the worst kind. It soon reached the attention of Henry Davenant, a member of King George I's inner circle. Davenant travelled to Godalming to examine the rabbits for himself and was also convinced as to the truth of Mary's story, returning to London with samples of the animals.

It appears that Howard became involved in Mary's hoax and he had Mary moved to Guildford, offering to give live demonstrations of her 'gift' to any disbeliever. He also wrote personal letters to various prominent surgeons, including to Nathaniel St André, the king's own surgeon.

The royal family were interested in the matter so much that the king sent his surgeon and Samuel Molyneux (the Prince of Wales' secretary) to investigate the matter. Arriving at Guildford on 15 November 1726, the two men witnessed Mary give birth to another rabbit before their very eyes. St André conducted experiments on the rabbit and upon Mary, and concluded that the story was true. A further two 'births' were made that same day, the final of which produced some rabbit skin and a rabbit's head that St André personally delivered.

The king then sent another surgeon, Cyciacus Ahlers, to Guildford. Ahlers was convinced from the outset that the entire story was a hoax, and conducted his own experiments on the rabbits, finding that the body parts had clearly been butchered with knives and also found pieces of plants in their droppings. With scepticism now growing stronger, Howard attempted to discredit Ahler's findings, but to little avail. Further experts were dispatched to make further investigations. The hoax was finally exposed on 4 December when it was found that Mary's husband had been purchasing young rabbits recently, and another person confessed to having been bribed to sneak a rabbit into Mary's chamber after being moved to Guildford.

Mary was arrested and questioned, but still maintained her story was true. However, after one of her investigators threatened to perform a painful operation on her, Mary confessed all: following her miscarriage, Mary had an accomplice insert the various animal parts into her womb and together invented the story of Mary becoming entranced by the rabbit in the field. The later 'births' were all the result of similar actions.

Mary was sent to a prison in London on a charge of being a 'vile cheat and imposter' before being brought before the court in January 1727. She was kept in prison for three months before being discharged due to the law not being clear as to what, if any, crime she had committed, and also because she had fallen ill during her imprisonment. Mary returned to Godalming and the following year gave birth to a daughter. She appears to have led a quiet and unremarkable life afterwards, although on 19 April 1740 a newspaper reported that 'The celebrated Rabbit woman of Godalmin in Surry [sic], was committed to Guildford Gaol, for receiving stolen goods'. She died in 1763 and was buried in the town on 13 January.

Treacle Mines

A once popular joke, probably meant as a means to trick the gullible along the lines of fireproof matches and left-handed screwdrivers, was that treacle was mined from the ground like oil or coal.

The joke originated in Victorian Chobham, when, it is said, 8,000 soldiers were camped on Chobham Common in advance of departing for the Crimean War in 1853. Before leaving, the soldiers decided that they would bury their treacle for safe keeping until they could return and retrieve it, but the stash was discovered by the villagers, who became known as the treacle miners.

There are some slight variations to the tale – as there are in all good folk tales – with some claiming that the treacle was buried when the camp was dismantled so that the soldiers didn't have to carry it away with them, while another version says that the treacle barrels were buried and forgotten about until they burst open after five decades, leading to sticky sweet ooze seeping out of the ground.

Above left: Chobham Common. (Don Cload)

Above right: An old cannon at Chobham. (Colin Smith)

The Giant Sisters

To the south and south-east of Guildford, approximately 2 miles apart, are the twin hilltop chapels of St Catherine and St Martha. Legend says that two giant sisters built the chapels using their own hands; the only tool they had to hand was a single hammer, which they tossed from one hill to the other as and when it was needed.

However, some sources state that St Martha's was originally known as The Martyr's or alternatively as St Thomas the Martyr's Chapel. In 1463, the chapel had fallen into a state of disrepair and the Prior of Newark offered forty days' indulgence (i.e. forty days relief from Purgatory after death) for any person who visited the chapel, performed certain prayers and made an offering towards the repairs. This is certainly an invention, since the name of St Martha is recorded long before this alleged story.

St Catherine's Hill also has its own separate legends, one of which is that this was where Sir Lancelot was tended by Elaine of Astolat after being wounded in a jousting tournament. St Catherine's is also said to have had an earlier name: Drake Hill, in reference to the folklore of a giant worm or fire drake that lived beneath the hill.

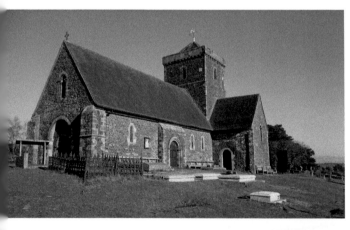

St Martha's Chapel. (Mark Percy)

Ruins of St Catherine's Chapel. (Mark Percy)

The Archbishop and the Pike

Perhaps one of the most famous sons of Guildford was Bishop George Abbot, Archbishop of Canterbury from 1611 until 1633. He was born in the town, where his father worked as a cloth merchant, and was taught at the local grammar school. Although he went on to have an illustrious career, a family legend gives a curious beginning to his life.

When his mother was pregnant with him, she had a dream that if she ate a pike her son would grow up to be a great man. Upon waking, his mother longed to satisfy this new strange craving and set about enquiring about where she could acquire such a fish. Without much luck, she carried out her usual daily duty of fetching water in a pail from the river and in so doing scooped out a pike. She took it home, cooked it, and ate it to the last morsel. The story spread across the town and attracted the attention of several of Guildford's wealthy inhabitants, who desired to be present at the birth. Of these, three suitable men were chosen and went on to sponsor George's education throughout his childhood.

George never forgot his roots and endowed Abbot's Hospital in the town, and when he died in Croydon on 4 August 1633, his body was brought back to Guildford for burial within Holy Trinity Church.

Above left: George Abbot's birthplace, now a pub. (Colin Smith)

Above right: Statue of George Abbot. (Colin Smith)

Above: Abbot Hospital, Guildford.
(Gaius Cornelius)

Left: George Abbot's tomb, Guildford.
(Jack1956)

The Vanished Heart

A strange relic was once housed within No.25 High Street, Guildford, formerly the home of the Martyr family. The house, now converted into a fast-food outlet close to the charming little bridge over the River Wey, was once decorated with wood panels under the windows and delicate iron railings outside. It also was home to a religious relic for about a hundred years until it mysteriously went missing in the early nineteenth century.

The story begins with the death of Peter des Roches, Bishop of Winchester, at his home in Farnham Castle on 9 June 1238. His body was taken for burial at Winchester, but his heart was first removed and taken to Waverley Abbey, near Farnham. In about 1730, the heart was accidentally excavated among the now ruined abbey, and was brought to Guildford. For reasons unknown, it entered into the possession of John Martyr, who kept it safe in its original lead case. However, about a century later the case (and the heart concealed inside) vanished – no record of how it vanished or where it now lies has been recorded.

Former Martyr family home. (N. Chadwick)

The Bullbeggars

It would appear that many centuries ago, in a time long since forgotten, the inhabitants of Woking were terrorised by evil goblins living in the countryside; if someone got too near (especially at night), the bullbeggars would leap out and chase the poor, unsuspecting victim all the way back to his house. The mischievous creatures would also sometimes lure their victims by pretending to be a person lying injured on the road, before jumping up and terrorising their prey.

The legend lives on in Woking with the naming of Bullbeggars Lane in the Horsell area of the town. It would seem that Godstone was also plagued by the little imps, since that village also has a Bullbeggars Lane.

Bullbeggars Lane, Horsell. (Alan Hunt)

Martian Invasion

Among Woking's famous residents was the science fiction and horror writer H. G. Wells, who moved to the town in 1895, living at 'Lynton' (now No. 141) Maybury Road. He lived there only for about eighteen months, but worked on some of his best known books while residing in town, including *The Invisible Man*, *The Time Machine*, *The Island of Dr. Moreau*, and *The War of the Worlds*.

Wells, who was very familiar with Sussex and Surrey, set many of his books in these two counties, and it was at Woking that he got inspiration for *War of the Worlds* while exploring the local countryside. In the novel, the Martians landed at Horsell Common and the narrator, who lived in Woking, tells the story of how the tripods first terrorised their way across north Surrey, and then were finally defeated by bacteria.

The novel, and Well's connection to Woking, are commemorated in the town with a series of four public art installations, including a Martian pod half embedded in the pavement, and a 7-metre-tall stainless steel tripod.

Above left: Martian tripod, Woking. (Len Williams)

Above right: H. G. Wells memorial, Woking. (Nick Richards)

Martian pod at Woking. (Nick Richards)

Horsell Common, site of the Martian landing. (Colin Smith)

The Haunting of Hillside House

Ghost stories and tales of hauntings have generally been avoided in this book. However, an exception has been made for what is a particularly unusual set of circumstances surrounding 'Hillside' in Egham.

This house, which fronts onto the A30 and has since been converted into apartments, does not look like a typical haunted house. Yet, it was subject to three separate lawsuits to prove or disprove its alleged supernatural activities between 1904 and 1907. The then owner of the house, Charles Arthur Barrett, brought the first claim in 1904 for damages against Stephen Phillips and various newspapers for circulating statements that his house was haunted by the ghost of a child murderer.

Barrett had purchased the property in 1890 and let it out for rent to various tenants without problem for thirteen years. However, in 1903 Phillips took on

"HILLSIDE," EGHAM

Hillside House, Egham. (*Haunted Houses*)

the tenancy and complained that he heard strange noises that he thought were the sounds of a child being strangled and doors opening by themselves. He became so terrified that he left the house before his tenancy ran out and took up residence in a local hotel instead. The following year, an account of Phillips' experiences was printed in the *Daily Express*, leading to the court case. Phillips and the other defendants settled the claim out of court by paying Barrett £200.

All went quiet until the *Daily Mail* reprinted the story in 1906. In this version, it was said that Phillips' young daughter saw an old man walking about the house, although they were the only tenants. It was supposed that the man had been a farmer who had, half a century earlier, killed a child nearby. The story once again made it difficult for Barrett to rent out his house.

In this second round of litigation, which did make it in front of the judge, Phillips said he secured the services of an expert to investigate the haunting, and it was he who told Phillips that the strange noises and opening doors was the result of the child victim's spirit. Phillips' QC questioned whether it was the fact that the house sat upon a busy road that deterred tenants rather than the ghosts. Unbelievably, the case went to the jury, who returned a verdict in favour of the plaintiff, Mr Barrett, for £90 damages against the newspapers that printed the story.

This was not the end of the affair since the defendants successfully appealed the decision in 1907 and the verdict was overturned – in the eyes of the law, the house was indeed haunted.

The house was eventually let out to a local police officer, who, when questioned, was of the opinion that the ghosts were actually just rats in the walls.

A3 Ghost Crash

It is not just old tales that form the history of Surrey; some much more recent events have spawned their own urban legends that have entered into the local folklore. In fact, it was only in 2018 that the A3 at Burpham was named as one of the UK's most haunted stretches of highway, owing to an event that occurred there in 2002.

The event that led to this strange 'honour' happened on 11 December 2002, when someone reported seeing a car lose control and crash off the road near the emergency slip road. The police arrived on the scene and conducted a search, but could not find any evidence that such a crash had occurred. At least, not at first.

Eventually, a dark red Vauxhall Astra was found almost hidden in a ditch and overgrown by brambles and other small woodland shrubs. There was no way that such a quantity of plant life could possibly have grown within a matter of a few hours. In fact, there was five months worth of growth blanketing the car.

Stranger still, the remains of the driver was found nearby and had also clearly been in position for quite some time. Tests revealed the identity of the man as an individual that was wanted by the Metropolitan Police for robbery, and had been missing since the middle of July.

Had the eyewitness observed some kind of time warp or ghostly replay of the crash that occurred earlier in the year? This question has divided people ever since, although the official opinion is that the location of the crash meant that it was simply not discovered until much later, and there was nothing supernatural about its discovery, although this explanation ignores the eyewitness report of the crash in December 2002.

Close to the site of the 'ghost crash' on the A3. (David Howard)

A Sprightly Centenarian

Within the churchyard of St John the Evangelist's Church at Merrow lies Walter Broke. According to his headstone, he reached the age of 107 years before he died in 1603. More impressive than his age is the local story that he celebrated his 100th birthday by walking from Merrow to London in a day – a distance of nearly 30 miles!

The Pyrford Stone

On a roadside verge at the entrance to Pyrford Court on Church Hill is a stone that is the subject of an unusual set of stories. Easy to miss due to its unremarkable size (less than a metre tall and just 40 centimetres wide), the Pyrford Stone's plaque labels it as merely a 'boundary stone ... from before the Norman Conquest and is possibly a prehistoric standing stone. Situated on this corner since time immemorial, it was moved to its present position during road widening'. This smooth, isolated stone is almost featureless bar a small cross etched into the top of it and some think it may have been a simple memorial stone for some long-forgotten person killed at the spot; in the years before the First World War it was custom in Surrey for the police to 'kick a cross' (i.e. draw a cross with their foot) in the dirt at the location of where someone was killed on the road.

More interesting is the legend that the Pyrford Stone moves about on its own at midnight and is also said to spin around when the Pyrford church clock strikes midnight. This last is perhaps one of those stories invented to mock gullible travellers, since St Nicholas' Church does not have a clock.

Above left: The Pyrford Stone. (Simon Burchell)

Above right: Modern stone circle at the Nuffield Health centre, Pyrford. (Peter Trimming)

The Treasure Stone

On the outskirts of Chertsey is another of those old hilltop chapels, now in ruins, that we first met near Guildford. Chertsey's St Anne's Hill, however, has a legend of a treasure stone – or, at least, it used to.

Near the top of the hill is a natural spring around which a rough stone and brick 'grotto' has been built. In the late seventeenth century there stood a huge stone nearby, known as the Devil's Stone. Buried beneath this monolith was an immense treasure, but the only snag was that the stone was so big that it could not be moved. It was also said to impart some mystical power upon the spring, which never froze over when others did.

The story of the immovable stone was proved to be unfounded when, at some time 'many years ago' (so writes Brayley in 1850), it was removed and destroyed.

St Anne's Hill. (Alan Hunt)

Blanche Heriot

The legendary heroine of Chertsey was first recorded in print by the Victorian novelist Albert Smith. Set in 1471, during the bitter Wars of the Roses, the story follows the fate of Blanche Heriot and her lover, Neville Audley. Edward IV had just regained his throne for the Yorkist cause, and Neville found himself a wanted man, for he had fought against the king. Upon returning to Chertsey, he planned to flee to Europe, but was arrested by the king's men before he could do so. In the struggle he killed one of the soldiers and managed to reach Chertsey Abbey to seek sanctuary. Unfortunately for Neville, his captors ignored the custom and took him away into custody to await execution the next day, when the town's curfew bell tolled.

Site of Chertsey Abbey. (JohnArmagh)

Neville, while away in battle, had shown mercy to a Yorkist nobleman and in return the nobleman gave Neville his ring as a token of gratitude. Whilst Neville was locked away awaiting his execution, a friend took the ring and promised to go to London to seek out the nobleman, who was to return the favour and save Neville's life.

This friend carried out his task, but was slow in returning to Chertsey; with just five minutes to go until the curfew bell was due to toll, he was still half a mile distant. It fell to Blanche to take action; knowing her lover's life depended upon the execution being delayed long enough for the ring bearer to return, she raced to the bell tower, climbed to the top and crawled underneath the bell, clinging onto the clapper for dear life and preventing it from ringing. In the nick of time, the pardon arrived and Neville was released; he and Blanche were married shortly afterwards. Of course, they lived happily ever after.

The story is commemorated by a bronze statue of Blanche and the curfew bell in Chertsey, and a unit at the local St Peter's Hospital is also named in her honour.

Statue of Blanche Heriot in Chertsey. (Chemical Engineer)

West Clandon Dragon

Set within the south wall of St Peter and St Paul's Church at West Clandon is an upside-down sundial and close by, within the grounds of Clandon Park, is Hinemihi – a Maori meeting house originally built by the Ngati Hinemihi tribe at Te Wairoa in 1880. These are not the most intriguing things about this village, however, since in a non-descript field nearby a fierce battle between unusual enemies is said to have once taken place.

A large serpent or dragon used to live in a rural country lane in the village. A soldier condemned to death for desertion promised, on condition that his life is spared, to rid the village of their troublesome dragon. The proposition was consented to and, taking his faithful dog with him, the soldier set out to find the beast. The dragon was encountered in a field belonging to the church called Deadacre, and the soldier's dog bravely lunged at the serpent, pinning it with his jaws so that the soldier could come in to make the *coup de grâce* with his bayonet.

More recently, the dragon returned to West Clandon when it was cut into the chalk embankment alongside the A426 at the West Clandon crossroads to mark the queen's silver jubilee in 1977. By 1990, however, it had disappeared to the vegetation, but was later restored. The village sign also bears a depiction of the dragon being attacked by the soldier's dog.

The upside-down sundial at West Clandon Church. (Colin Smith)

The Silent Pool

Officially the Sherbourne Ponds, this pond just off the A25 near Albury has been a popular site for visitors since the Victorian era, and is considered by some to be a sacred site due to a medieval legend of murder.

The story is that the pool was the favourite haunt of a beautiful peasant girl, who used to bathe in it regularly. Then one day King John was passing by and came across this young woman. Overcome by malice, the king drove his horse at her, forcing her back into the pond. In her attempt to escape, she lost her footing and fell into deeper water and drowned.

Having witnessed the event, the woman's brother tried to rescue her, but also came into difficulties and met with the same fate; and there the two of them lie to this very day. The murdered woman is said to rise from the water at midnight.

The name of The Silent Pool was later assigned owing to the eerie silence (or near silence) of the pond, despite being only a short distance from a busy highway; it is said that not even the birds will sing in the trees surrounding the waters.

The Silent Pool. (Alan Hunt)

The Mysterious Case of the Mystery Writer

Close by the Silent Pool is another popular visitor hotspot: Newlands Corner. It was here, in December 1926, that one of the world's most famous writers disappeared.

On the morning of 4 December, a Morris Cowley was found half buried in a bush on the edge of a quarry. Inside were some clues as to its owner: an old dressing case, a fine fur coat, and a driving licence bearing the name of Agatha Christie. The writer herself was nowhere to be seen.

Newlands Corner. (Banalities)

A 1926 Morris Cowley, similar to that owned by Agatha Christie. (Martin Vähning)

Over the next few days the story swept the public imagination; newspapers were splashing it across their front pages. The belief was that Agatha was dead – probably by her own hand – and the numerous gravel pits and woods were searched – even the Silent Pool was dredged, but all to no avail.

Then, the idea struck that maybe Agatha had been murdered. Information came to the fore that Agatha's husband, Archie Christie, had been having an affair with another woman and, on the night before her car was discovered, he had been staying with his girlfriend at a house nearby.

On the 12th, a mass public gathering took place at Newlands Corner to hunt for Agatha's body. Approximately 2,000 people turned up, and bloodhounds were brought in, but still to no avail. The dreaded news that everyone expected to hear failed to materialise.

The mystery was blown open, however, on 13 December 1926, when two members of staff at the Hydro Hotel in Harrogate informed the police that they believed Agatha Christie was staying at the hotel. For the eleven days of her

Chilworth station, where Agatha departed for London. (Stefan Czapski)

disappearance, she had in fact been staying in Yorkshire, but later reported that she had no memory of what had happened.

Agatha appeared to have suffered from some kind of nervous breakdown; in April she had lost her beloved mother, and then in August her husband informed her that he had been having an affair with a younger woman and wanted a divorce. With some apparent intent to leave a series of clues, Agatha had left her home at Sunningdale, in Berkshire, in her car and headed the 20 miles to Newlands Corner, just 5.5 miles from where her husband was staying with his girlfriend. Leaving her car perched on the edge of a gravel pit, she left the above-mentioned items as clues to let the police know that it was her car when they found it.

Unbeknown to the police, Agatha then made the short journey on foot to Chilworth station to catch the morning train to Waterloo. In London, she visited Harrod's to leave a ring for repair, giving the name of the hotel in Harrogate where she intended to stay, albeit in the name of her husband's girlfriend as a red herring. She then caught another train to Harrogate and checked into the hotel.

When the police were eventually tipped off by the hotel staff, Archie went to Yorkshire to collect her. The media had also turned out and surrounded the hotel's entrance, and so it was decided to try and sneak out a side entrance. However, a *Daily Mail* photographer was waiting and snapped pictures of a blank-faced Agatha being escorted by her husband. It was Archie who first suggested that Agatha was suffering from a 'fugue state,' and Agatha never revealed what really went on during those eleven days in December 1926. The fact of the clues that were carefully left, and the location of where she left her car to be found, all indicate that there was some kind of design in her actions.

The media frenzy did not let up, and, for Agatha, Britain was becoming like a prison where every intimate detail of her life was being splashed around for 'entertainment'. However, she found a new freedom through travel, and spent several years exploring Europe, North Africa and the Middle East. Meeting a new husband in Iran, Agatha went on to write many of her best-known Poirot novels in the years following her disappearance.

The False Tomb

There is some debate as to whether Cranleigh is a town or a village; those who live there proudly contend that it is the largest village in England, others regard it merely as a town that has retained some of its village characteristics.

The village does, however, have a splendid church with a neat churchyard enclosed by an old brick wall. Within this churchyard, so an old story would have us believe, was an altar tomb that held a secret – it was a secret hiding place for smugglers' contraband.

One story told to the late local historian, Gertrude Jekyll, spoke of how kegs of brandy would be concealed within the empty tomb and collected late at night when the coast was clear. In one story, some excisemen hid in the church porch to await the smugglers in action, but lost their nerve when the smugglers did arrive to collect their illicit bounty.

Tombs in Cranleigh churchyard. (John Salmon)

St Nicholas' Church, Cranleigh. (John Salmon)

The Anchoress and the Pope

Close to the altar inside St James' Church at Shere you may notice the remains of a quatrefoil and squint window in the wall. On the outside wall you will also find a small metal plaque with the intriguing inscription: 'Site of the cell of Christine Carpenter, Anchoress of Shere 1329'.

An anchoress was a type of religious hermit who volunteered to be sealed for life within a small cell attached to a church. In Shere, this was Christine Carpenter who, in 1329, asked the Bishop of Winchester for permission to become an anchoress. Several persons of repute were brought forward to swear as to Christine's good character and her virginity. The bishop assented and a small anchorite cell was built onto the north side of the chancel. Aside from the small squint window looking upon the altar inside the church, the only other means of communication with the outside world was a door to allow her to receive Holy Communion. With great ceremony and ritual, Christine was shut inside her new home in July 1329.

However, after a couple of years, Christine seemed to have had a change of heart and was found to have broken out of her cell (and therefore broken her sacred vows) and was under threat of excommunication – a very serious penalty at the time.

Plaque
commemorating
Christine Carpenter.
(SuzanneKn)

Perhaps it was this threat that led to Christine considering recommitting herself to her vows. She wrote to Pope John XXII in 1332 (or rather had the bishop write to him on her behalf) expressing her desire to become an anchoress once again. The letter argued that Christine's wishes should be fulfilled, her transgressions against the Church forgiven and that she should be allowed to re-enter the cell, on condition that she suffered penance for her behaviour.

The Pope gave his blessing, and Christine entered the anchorite cell for the second time (presumably in 1332). This time, however, the door was sealed off and blocked up so that she could never leave. Instead, the quatrefoil window was added into the side of the chancel to allow her to receive Communion, and a small window was built into the outer wall to allow food and water to be passed in, and her wastes to be passed out, but too small for her to be able to climb out of.

It is believed that Christine did indeed spend the rest of her life locked in isolation within her small, dark cell. It is not known when she died, and since there are no more records indicating that she left the cell again, it is presumed that she died and was buried within her cell.

Site of the anchorite cell, Shere. (BabelStone)

Quatrefoil and squint windows at Shere. (BabelStone)

The Head in the Crypt

The vault under St Mary the Virgin's Church in West Horsley is supposed to contain the head of one of the Elizabethan era's most famous personalities: Sir Walter Raleigh.

When the explorer was executed in London on the morning of 29 October 1618, his severed head was placed into a red velvet bag and was presented to his widow, Bess. While imprisoned in the Tower of London, Sir Walter had got his wife pregnant with their son, Carew; it is through him that West Horsley comes into the story.

Carew Raleigh came into possession of West Horsley Place in 1643, and brought his mother with him. Bess' love for her dead husband was so great that she had his head embalmed and kept it with her for the rest of her life, bringing it to West Horsley with her.

West Horsley Place. (Colin Smith)

When Bess died at West Horsley Place in 1647, the head was placed in a cupboard and there it remained until 1660 when illness struck the house. Carew's three young children fell ill and died, and were buried together under a chapel within St Mary the Virgin's Church. Before the vault was sealed, however, the head was supposedly also interred with the children.

The story fast forwards to 1703. By now the house had come into the possession of William Nicholas. In this year, his wife, Penelope, was killed when the chimney fell through the roof during a storm that wreaked death and destruction across much of southern England. The vault in the church was reopened to take Penelope's body, and in so doing a head was found.

The tomb is unmarked today, but the story does not end here. Almost four centuries later, in 2018, a red velvet bag was discovered hidden in the attic of West Horsley Place during repair work. Initial analysis has revealed this bag to be of the correct date and style to fit in with the legend, although, at the time of writing, no conclusive proof has been found one way or another as to if it is *the* bag that once held Sir Walter's head. Further testing and analysis is ongoing, so perhaps one day this legend may turn out to be true.

Nicholas family memorial near the unmarked Raleigh vault. (John Salmon)

The Hermit of Painshill Park

Painshill Park came to prominence under the ownership of Charles Hamilton, who had the expansive gardens decorated with an astonishing variety of chapels, grottoes, temples, mock castles, waterfalls and ruins. Among these was also a hermitage with a real live hermit living in it – or at least that was the plan.

However, the hermit proved to be somewhat of a failure. Having been offered the sum of £700 (2021: £61,079) by Hamilton to live a simple life in his specially built cell, sleeping on a mat, deprived of a toilet and forbidden to speak a word, the hermit decided to abandon his post after just three weeks and was found drinking in the pub. He didn't get his money, but at least he didn't have to spend the rest of his life (or until such time as Hamilton got bored of him) locked within his small wooden tree house on the borders of the park.

While most of the other follies in the park, including the crystal-lined grottoes, survive, the original hermitage was left to fall into ruin and was finally broken up for firewood during the Second World War. A modern replica was built in 2004 and is open for visitors to experience what it would have been like to live in it.

The Hermitage, Painshill Park. (AndyScott)

Crystal Arch, Painshill Park. (AndyScott)

The Crystal Grotto, Painshill Park. (AndyScott)

The Surrey Parakeets

If you visit Cobham's parks and woods at certain times of the year, you may be presented with the sight (or more likely sounds) of a flock of bright green tropical birds that have no place being in Surrey. The question is how did they get here?

This is a mystery that has been unanswered, and has given rise to several divergent theories. The most basic is that the birds escaped from London Zoo in the 1960s and headed a short distance south before deciding they had found a suitable location to set up nest. Some people will have you believe that they were released into the wild by Jimi Hendrix in the 1960s, or that the original birds escaped from Shepperton Studios during the making of *The African Queen* in 1951. Others say that they fled north from Spain in the 1930s when the civil war raged there, or escaped during customs checks at Heathrow Airport. Most sources will tell you that the birds are simply the offspring of pets that escaped over the years, although why they all seem to congregate around the Cobham area is anyone's guess.

In truth, parakeets have been known to be living wild in this part of England since 1855, and as many as 50,000 are now believed to be living in Surrey.

A Surrey parakeet. (Ian Capper)

The First Honeymoon

It is often the case that new trends are started by celebrities. This is no truer than in a new fad set by William the Marshall at Stoke D'Abernon in 1189 that has stood the test of time and is still a very popular ritual for newly-weds the world over.

This small village on the outskirts of Cobham is perhaps not the sort of place that many people would have high up on their list of potential honeymoon venues, charming though it is. However, it is where the custom was 'invented' more than 830 years ago.

William Marshal, 1st Earl of Pembroke, had a distinguished career serving five different kings from Henry II until Henry III, and married his very young wife, Isabelle de Clare, in 1189. Isabelle was the daughter of the King of Leinster, and their marriage made William one of the richest men in any of the kingdoms that now make up the UK. Upon their marriage, the owner of Stoke Manor, who also paid for the wedding, offered the couple his house in which to spend the first few nights of their marriage.

Parkside School, formerly Stoke Manor. (Colin Smith)

The Saracen and the Ring

Originally known as the White Hart, there was once a pub in Great Bookham with the rather mystifying name of Saracen & Ring from 1819 until it closed in the 1890s.

A mid-nineteenth-century landlord of the pub gave this story as to the origin of the name. During one of the many wars of the Crusades in the Holy Land, Sir William Dawney found himself face-to-face in combat with a Saracen prince. During the battle at Acon, the Saracen's head was cleaved from his neck. Once the battle was fought and won, the prince's possessions were looted, including, among many other jewels, a very valuable ring. Thus, the pub was named in honour of this warrior's victory, since his descendents had a house near to the village.

Another account of the legend says that after killing the prince, Sir William killed a ferocious lion and cut off the paw as a gift to present to Richard I. The king, upon receiving the paw, removed his own ring and presented it as a token to Sir William in honour of the event.

The pub has long since been converted into a residential house, although in one final ironic twist, the first buyer of the property after it was closed in the 1890s was Mary Chrystie, a renowned temperance campaigner.

Former Saracen & Ring pub, Great Bookham. (Colin Smith)

Ockley Roses

Until relatively recently, Ockley had its own village tradition that is both heart-warming and yet tinged with sadness. Within the churchyard of St Margaret's Church, for several centuries it was the custom that red roses were planted on the grave of one's sweetheart. In fact, writing in the late seventeenth century, Aubrey relates how he observed one woman tend the roses on the grave of her beloved, whom had died before they could get married, and that she had spent twenty years caring for the grave with great love and affection, having declined to marry another man.

The rose bushes still existed in abundance all across the churchyard into the twentieth century, although today there are but a few – if any at all – still remaining.

Above left: St Margaret's Church, Ockley. (Dave Kelley)

Above right: Ockley churchyard – not a rose to be seen. (Hassocks5489)

Battle of Aclea

Ockley is hardly the spot you would consider when thinking about great battles. Yet, it is at Ockley where it is believed that one of the greatest battles of the Viking era was fought.

Long before King Harold fell at Hastings, a huge Viking armada arrived off the Kent coast in AD 851. The 350 longboats carried 15,000 fierce warriors, who sacked and pillaged their way through Canterbury and into London. Now, the only target left before them was Winchester – the capital of the kingdom of Wessex. Crossing the Thames, the invading Viking army moved into Surrey, and it was here that Ethelwulf, King of Wessex, would meet them on the battlefield.

At this time, most of the Weald of Sussex and Surrey was a wild forest, not fit for any sort of fighting, but at Ockley the forest gave way to open countryside, and so at Ockley the battle was fought – most likely on the higher ground around Leith Hill.

Ethelwulf spread his army across the line of advance and the tales tell of the most violent battle that spilled blood 'ankle deep' on the ground, and littered the hills with thousands of dead and dying Vikings. Not a single one was said to have escaped with his life; the victory was complete and Ethelwulf had saved both the kingdom and the fate of the Saxons. The Vikings did not attempt to make another invasion of the British Isles for another fourteen years. Even until the mid-twentieth century, locals would assert that the water running down off Leith Hill after a rain shower would be stained red.

Above left: Looking north-west across Ockley. (Lewis Clarke)

Above right: Leith Hill from Ockley, the supposed battlefield. (Eddy Greenfield)

The Devil's Causeway

Another of the old legends that have assigned pre-Christian features in the landscape with the devil has grown up with regards to the old Roman road of Stane Street, which used to run through Dorking on its way from Chichester to London. In the town, it took a course through what is now St Martin's churchyard, and parts of it have been uncovered over the centuries through the digging of graves. In particular, the hardcore of flints and pebbles would be dug up. Yet, legend states that flints do not occur naturally within a 7-mile radius of the town, and the pebbles are such as found on the coast. To explain their presence in Dorking, a story was created assigning the Roman road as a causeway made by the devil.

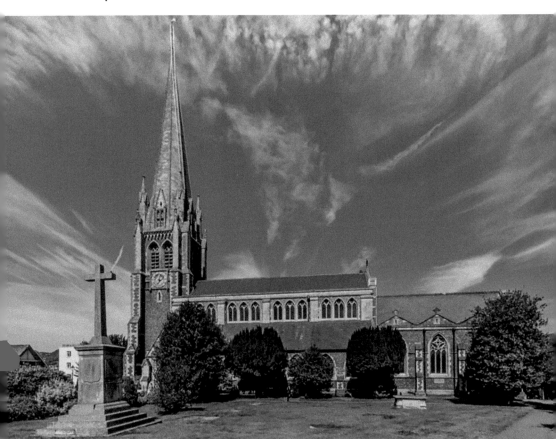

St Martin's Church and churchyard, Dorking. (Ian Capper)

The Valley of the Shadow
of Death

In 1734, Jonathan Tyers purchased the Denbies Estate and converted it into a weekend retreat. Tyers was known at the time for founding a popular pleasure gardens beside the Thames in Kensington, but his vision for Denbies was somewhat different to the cheerful Vauxhall Garden he created in London.

At the time, the estate consisted of a farmhouse and fields, and Tyers set about redesigning the grounds in his own taste. First, he converted the farm buildings into a large house, and then went about creating a Gothic garden, which he named The Valley of the Shadow of Death. The macabre landscaping was supposed to be a constant reminder to guests of their own mortality (although one has to wonder how many guests he did receive). At the centre of the garden was a small temple covered in morbid inscriptions. Inside, a clock struck every minute to remind visitors of the constant passage of time and the relentless approach of death; alongside it, in two alcoves, were two life-size paintings of a Christian and a non-Christian in their death throes. In addition, at the end of the path leading to the temple were two pedestals mounted with skulls.

Jonathan died in 1767, and the property was inherited by his two sons. Remarkably, the death garden at Denbies was retained for over a century before a later owner took possession and removed all traces of the temple and gardens.

Denbies from Dorking station. (*A Handbook of Dorking*)

The Tunning of Elynour Rummyng

Close to the Guildford Road bridge in Leatherhead stands The Running Horse pub. This charming timber-framed building nestled between the modern red-brick apartment blocks and offices is at the centre of a Tudor poem recalling the life of the landlady some five centuries ago.

The name of the pub is believed to be a play on the original name, Rummin's House, and was run by one Elynor Rummyn. As well as caring and providing for her family, Elynor would have run the alehouse single-handedly, including brewing her own beer in the pub's garden.

The Running Horse, Leatherhead. (Robert Eva)

We probably would not have known much about Elynor if it wasn't for the fact that a man by the name of John Skelton stopped off for a drink one night. Skelton, however, turned out to be Henry VIII's poet laureate, and he wrote a rather disparaging poem about Elynor.

The poem, running for over 200 lines, is too long to reproduce in full, but includes this vivid description of his host:

> Her lithely leer
> Is nothing clear,
> But ugly of cheer,
> Droopy and drowsy,
> Scurvy and lousy;
> Her face all bowsy,
> Comely crinkled,
> Wondrously wrinkled,
> Like a roast pigs ear,
> Bristled with hair.

The poem is mostly a personal attack on Elynor, and while it may come across quite humorous, its meaning was deadly serious. It was intended as an attack on these so-called 'ale wives', and to keep women 'in their place' for centuries to come.

Portrait of Elynor Rummyn. (P. L. Chadwick)

Penny for the Corpse

Not too far from the Running Horse once stood the Swan Hotel, now demolished. Here existed an unusual belief that the carrying of a dead body can establish a lawful right of way. Fearing that such a right of way would be created through his property, a former landlord of the Swan began to charge a fee of one penny should anyone desire to carry a body through his brewery yard in order to ensure that it remained as private property.

The town also has another legend regarding rights of way concerning the church. Inside St Mary and St Nicholas' Church, any visitor will quickly notice that the entrance into the tower is offset significantly from the axis of the nave, and the tradition for this architectural anomaly is that the tower had to be built out of alignment in order to avoid blocking a right of way.

Site of the former Swan Hotel, Leatherhead. (Ian Capper)

Magic Water

Between Cobham Road and the River Mole at Leatherhead is the former millpond. Measuring about 270 metres long and 70 metres wide, its size is impressive, but for one visitor in the years following the First World War, it was 'unlike any other pond I know'. Described as an 'intense clear green,' patches of deeper colour could be observed among the weeds. These patches, we are informed, appeared to move when observed. When stones were thrown into these pools, they 'disappear as if they were swallowed'. Furthermore, when the stone hit the surface of the pond it sent out the usual ripples, but after a few seconds, when the stone was still just about visible, another mysterious ripple 'a mere ring of light … leaps out apparently from the side of the pool a foot or so under water'. When this reached out and touched the stone, the stone disappeared; 'there is no stirring of mud … it merely disappears into an invisible mouth in the green'. On top of this, we are told that the pond never freezes, even in the hardest of winters.

The 'magic water' of the millpond. (Ian Capper)

Lord Hope and the Hellhound

Despite being called Betchworth Castle, the now ruined house is actually on the north-western outskirts of Brockham and is surrounded almost entirely by a golf course. The property has a long and fascinating history, originating as a Norman earthwork fortification before being built as a stone castle in the late twelfth century, and then rebuilt as a fortified house in the mid-fifteenth century. The castle passed through various hands until becoming uninhabited in the nineteenth century, and left to fall into ruin.

Like many ruins Betchworth has its own legends of hauntings. The best known of these is the tale of Lord Hope. Although the castle was owned by men named Hope towards the end of its life, it has never been occupied by a Lord Hope. However, Lord Hope is said to have been alarmed by an intruder and gave chase. Having finally hunted down and captured the prowler, Lord Hope ran his sword through him and killed the man. Unfortunately, it was only now that Lord Hope saw who the man was; he was no intruder, but his own son. Lord Hope's ghost now wanders the ruins still full of remorse at having murdered his own heir.

Another particularly interesting legend is that the castle is haunted by a Black Dog (sometimes better known as a Hellhound, Death Hound, or Black Shuck). These creatures are said to be very large dogs (sometimes as large as a horse), covered entirely in black fur and often with red, glowing eyes. They are also known for their loud, blood-curdling howls, but it is only if you should see one that you need to worry, for they are omens of imminent death. Fortunately, the one at Betchworth is said to only show himself at night.

Above left: The crumbling ruins. (AndyScott)

Above right: Betchworth Castle ruins. (AndyScott)

A Wartime Mystery

Air raids were not at all unusual over Surrey for most of the war, and as a result hundreds of bombs were dropped all across the county. Of these, six fell harmlessly in woodland on Brockham Hill, and other than leaving behind a set of large craters would have been but a minor footnote in the village's history.

Then, in 1947, these otherwise unremarkable craters were visited by a local botanist and one of them was found to be sprouting unusual plants. In total, twenty-five different species were growing in this crater, none of which were known to have ever been present in the British Isles before.

Despite the best efforts to keep the craters a secret, the story leaked out a few years later, and in 1950 experts from all over descended on Brockham Hill to investigate. The mystery only grew deeper as the species were further indentified – they were all native to south and central Europe. The initial theory proposed was that the seeds had somehow become mixed into the bomb's explosives or had become attached to the casing. This was soon discredited: in such an event the seeds would almost certainly have been rendered unviable in the explosions and the seeds originated from as far apart as Greece, Yugoslavia and Austria.

A second idea suggested was that migrating birds had deposited the seeds, but this was also soon dismissed due to the highly localised growing pattern, and the wide variety of species growing in the crater. The botanists decided to leave the plants alone to see if they would propagate themselves, but within a month of the story going public they had all disappeared – presumably either died or were dug up. The mystery was never solved.

Brockham Hills.
(David Howard)

The Buckland Shag

The road between Buckland and Reigate is now a major highway, but it was originally a rural coaching lane. Close to Buckland the road crosses over the small Shag Brook, and until 1757, an unusual stone was embedded within the riverbank.

The story of this stone begins with the beautiful daughter of a local yeoman who was wooed by the owner of Buckland Manor. The courting couple made it their habit to walk this road as they swore their undying love for each other, but then one night, when the moon was full, the 'gentleman' made his real intention known; it wasn't a relationship with this young woman he was after, but he had more lustful desires – what today would be termed a 'one-night stand'.

The Shag Brook at Buckland. (N. Chadwick)

The woman was so shocked by this revelation that she fell dead at his feet. So distraught at what he had caused, the gentleman pulled a dagger from his pocket and plunged it into his own heart. The following morning a traveller passed by the spot and saw that a large stone had appeared in the stream, with drops of blood still trickling into the clear water. Indeed, the stone, when it existed, was described as having a blood-red vein of iron ore running through the heart of it.

From this grew another legend. A hideous monster, described variously as resembling a horse, donkey, large dog or an ape-like creature, inhabited the stream and would wait for passers-by to cross it at night. Like a troll, any person daring to trip-trap across the Shag's bridge was fair game, and would be dragged into the water and eaten.

It fell to a villager, fed up of the creature, to take matters into his own hands. Having become rather drunk at Reigate Market, he made a wager that if he came across the Shag he would fight the beast with his trusty hawthorn cane. With the promise made, the villager arrived at the brook at the stroke of midnight. As expected, the gruesome Shag appeared before him and, as promised, the man struck the creature with his stick, but it merely passed through it unharmed. Now shocked into sobriety, the man about-turned and ran with the beast hot on his heels. It wasn't until the man got safely to his own front door that the creature vanished. However, it was too late for the man; although the Shag didn't get him, his shock was such that he died a week later.

The Buckland Shag was only finally vanquished when the local rector had the stone removed from the village in 1757 and had it thrown into the sea at Devon. Since this time, the Shag has not been seen haunting the road from Reigate to Buckland.

A variation on this myth was put forward by George Soane in 1847, who related the Shag as being the devil in disguise. The devil used to dance on the road near the brook, and despite being shot at and even pierced through the middle with a pitchfork, the locals could not persuade him to move on. Soane gave his own theory as to the existence of the beast – marsh gas. In some circumstances, marshes give off luminous gasses and Soane suggested that the rustic locals, knowing the legend of the Buckland Shag, imagined that these ethereal lights were to blame for the stories.

The Ewell Witch

Surrey was not the most fervent of places during the witch hunt hysteria of the sixteenth to early eighteenth centuries, bringing fewer than fifty individuals to trial for the crime of witchcraft, of which only twelve people were convicted.

Of these, one case has entered local folklore, that of Joan Butts at Ewell. On 5 October 1680 Mr and Mrs Tuers left their maid, Elizabeth Burgiss, in charge of the house while they went out. A little later, Joan Butts, 'a person that hath been for a long time suspected to be a Witch,' came to the house and asked the maid for an old pair of gloves. The maid knew of Joan's reputation and sent her away. A short time later, Joan appeared again at the house, asking for a pin for her neckcloth. This time Elizabeth consented and furnished Joan with a pin before sending her on her way. All was quiet for a fortnight until a rain of stones 'as big as a man's fist' suddenly began to fall in the yard of the Tuers' house, flying through the air and striking Elizabeth Burgiss repeatedly. The next day, Elizabeth began to complain of unbearable pains in her back, as though she was being pricked with pins.

Seeing the girl in such agony, Mr Tuers offered to inspect Elizabeth's back, and in so doing pulled out a large lump of clay full of pins from under her dress. Mr Tuers threw the clay into the fire and immediately Elizabeth's condition eased. However, Elizabeth began to suffer once again, and this time a Mr Waters was present and, upon reaching down the back of her dress, pulled out another lump of clay full of thorns. This was also burned in the fire, and Elizabeth was relieved of her pains.

The next morning, Elizabeth went to the cows to milk them, and in so doing saw a 'wretched old Caitiff' in Nonsuch Park, sitting among the thorn bushes and conversing with a demon. Elizabeth identified this 'caitiff' as Joan Butts, and rushed home to report what she had just seen. She had had enough, and that

Woodland at Nonsuch Park.
(Mike Pennington)

same night she packed for London. However, as she was getting her trunk, a dreadful scream shook the house. Mr Tuers raced up the stairs to the maid's room and found it in disarray. Elizabeth said that Joan had been in her room, but Mr Tuers couldn't see anyone else except Elizabeth.

From that point on, other manifestations occurred in the house, with items being seen to be thrown at the maid by an invisible hand whenever she passed through the house. Elizabeth decided to leave Ewell for her mother's house at Ashtead. On her journey, she was constantly bombarded by flying stones, but pressed on and reached the house on 9 October, only to find it in a mess, with acorns and nuts flying through the air around it. For several days items would suddenly disappear, or fly through the air, injuring whomsoever they hit.

On the 18th, a fair was held at Ewell, and Elizabeth's mother attended in the hope of seeing Joan Butts. See her she did; the mother immediately fell upon Joan and 'so evilly Treated her, that she fetch out some of her Hellish Hellish Blood.'

On the previous day of the alleged visit to the Tuers' house, a young girl by the name of Mary Farborough fell suddenly ill at Ewell, and the doctor suggested that witchcraft was responsible. The finger of suspicion was pointed at Joan, who appeared at the house that night; Mary died on 12 October and Joan was held accountable.

Joan Butts was later arrested, and brought to trial at Southwark on 23 March 1682 on the charge of bewitching Elizabeth Burridge [*sic*] in the above mentioned manner, and also bewitching to death Mary Farborough. A total of nineteen people were called as witnesses to the trial to testify against Joan, including Elizabeth Burgiss and her mother, Mr and Mrs Tuers and the parents of Mary Farborough. Joan pleaded not guilty to both cases, and the judge concurred; Joan was acquitted of all charges and released.

There are a number of other legends of witches in Surrey, although their tales are often more vague than that of Joan Butts at Ewell.

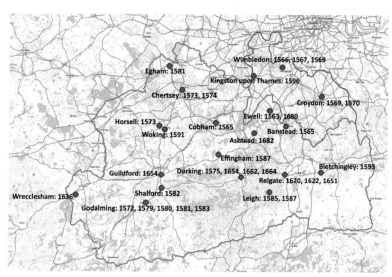

Map of alleged acts of witchcraft in Surrey. (OpenStreet Map)

St Cross Chapel

Reigate Heath Windmill is a Grade II* listed structure with an interesting history, but the most fascinating – and surprising – thing about it is that it is a consecrated church, believed to be the only windmill church in the world.

The windmill was built in around 1765, and worked continuously milling corn for approximately 100 years before ceasing operations in 1862. It stood vacant for almost two decades before the brick base was converted into a chapel of ease to St Mary's Church in Reigate town in 1880, with the first service taking place on 14 September.

Although the building was sold off to the surrounding Reigate Golf Club, the chapel remained open. In 1962, ownership passed to Reigate Borough Council, and although the chapel was retained, it appears to have been operated only intermittently, not least because of structural damage and extensive repairs needing to be carried out.

Following this renovation, the first church service was held on 18 October 1964, and from the following year services have been held there once a month during the summer ever since, including a wedding in the 1980s.

St Cross Chapel, Reigate Heath. (Allen Watkin)

The Baron's Cave

As at nearby Dorking, Reigate has its own sets of caves and tunnels with their own myths and legends. Close to the centre of the town are the ruins of Reigate Castle, which was built by William de Warenne, 2nd Earl of Surrey, in the decades following the Norman Conquest. The castle fell into the ownership of various noblemen in the centuries that followed. A mock medieval castle gateway was built on the site of the castle in 1777 by Richard Barnes in memory of William de Warenne.

Today, the only surviving part of the original castle is the so-called Baron's Cave, which had been dug into the rock underneath the castle. The history of this cave is not well documented, but a popular legend says that it was here that the rebellious barons met to draw up the terms of the Magna Carta in 1215.

Also of interest is the tunnel that runs underneath the castle; constructed in 1823, it is thought to have been the first road tunnel built in Europe, although today it is entirely pedestrianised. Additional tunnels and caves have been dug into the sides of it, serving various purposes over the years, including as air-raid shelters during the Second World War.

Reconstructed gate at Reigate Castle.
(Immanuel Giel)

Above: The Baron's Cave,
Reigate. (Dominic Alves)

Left: Reigate Tunnel.
(MartynDavies)

A Modern Spring-Heel Jack

A short distance south of Reigate Castle is Reigate Priory and its impressive park. The priory has an equally impressive history incorporating monks, Tudor kings and queens, Churchill, and Field Marshal Montgomery.

However, it was an event in April 1910 that caused much panic in the town. The story began when Mr Oakshott, a sergeant in the local Territorial Army unit, was taking a walk through Priory Park when a man suddenly jumped out on him from the trees armed with a revolver. 'I could see by the hideous smile and the distortion of his countenance that he was mad,' reported Sergeant Oakshott, who decided the best course of action was to back away slowly until safely out of the park. Then he turned and ran for his house to collect his rifle and to phone the police. Returning shortly afterwards with his own gun, he saw the man again; the stranger stared at the sergeant before slinking back into the trees. The police still had not arrived, so Sergeant Oakshott returned home to phone them again; the park was surrounded, and a thorough search undertaken, but the man was not found.

In the days that followed, the stranger suddenly appeared out of nowhere to harass Mrs Winter and her child and, on 8 April, jumped out on a sailor and attacked him. Further extensive searches were made, but to no avail. Sergeant Oakshott furnished the police with a detailed description of the man: 'about forty years of age, with light hair and a slight greyish moustache. He had no hat, collar, or tie, but wore a brown jacket and greyish trousers'. On the same day that the sailor was assaulted, a man matching this description was also seen in Coulsdon, although the police lost all trace of him. As with the original Victorian Spring-Heel Jack, this modern incarnation was never apprehended and his identity remains unknown.

Reigate Priory. (Eddy Greenfield)

Martin Bormann

It is fair to say that more has been written about Martin Bormann (head of the Nazi Party, and Hitler's personal private secretary) and his alleged activities after the Second World War than his time serving as Hitler's right-hand man. Among the more unusual of these conspiracies is of an apparent connection to Reigate.

It is true that Reigate was an important military centre during the war, especially for intelligence work: the town was the headquarters for the South Eastern Regional Command (headed by Field Marshal Montgomery); it was the location of the regional headquarters for the Auxiliary Units (an underground resistance army set up in preparation for an invasion); and in Doods Road was a top-secret pigeon loft used for the conveyance of secret messages.

Returning to Martin Bormann, he was last seen alive on 2 May 1945 in Berlin. No trace of him was found after the war, and he was convicted in absentia at the Nuremburg Trials. Stories abounded throughout the next three decades of Bormann sightings in South America – and in Reigate. In 1972, a pair of skeletons were unearthed in Berlin and were identified as being Hitler's doctor, Ludwig Stumpfegger, and Martin Bormann; later DNA testing on the bones confirmed the identification.

However, despite the official line being that Bormann was killed in Berlin in May 1945, the conspiracies regarding an apparent escape from Germany never ceased. In 1995, the *News of the World* ran a story proclaiming that a man in Reigate named Peter Broderick-Hartley had in fact been none other than Martin Bormann. The following year, a book, *Op JB*, was published claiming that a plan was hatched, labelled as Operation James Bond and led by the book's author and Ian Fleming, in which a British Commando raid infiltrated Berlin and managed to extricate Bormann to England, where he ended up living in Wray Common Road in Reigate (close to Doods Road). The plan was said to have been carried out on the express orders of Churchill.

Safely holed away in Reigate, Bormann underwent debriefings before being allowed out in public. The purpose of his removal to the UK was so that he could be used to retrieve the Nazi gold that had been sent out of Germany during the war.

Other theories, however, state that Bormann was killed, but that a mysterious man from Reigate, named William Hornegold was recruited by the British Secret Service and 'disappeared'. However, soon afterwards, another man (who looked exactly like Bormann) appeared in his place. This man was, apparently, used as a body double to retrieve 95 per cent of the Nazi gold stashed in banks around the world. Later on, this gentleman took the name of Peter Broderick-Hartley and lived out the rest of his life in Wray Common Road until he died in 1989. His remains were interred in Redstone Cemetery.

Other variations on the story link the man seen in Reigate with sightings of 'Bormann' in Argentina and Paraguay during the 1950s and 1960s (he was forced to flee England on the orders of Prime Minister Anthony Eden when he feared that the KGB would discover the fact that Britain had been harbouring Nazis when the Soviet Premier was due to arrive on a state visit), or that the person in Reigate was actually Bormann's son, or even that the man in Reigate was indeed an exact double of Bormann (including having surgery to match Bormann's dental profile) and was taken on Operation James Bond as a stooge, and that he was murdered by Ian Fleming's commando unit once the gold was recovered, and that it was really *his* skeleton that was uncovered in Berlin in 1972.

Wray Common Road, Reigate, supposedly home of Martin Bormann. (Ian Capper)

Holy Gabriel

The children's game Follow My Leader had its own version unique to Meadvale. The game is a simple one: a 'leader' is chosen from a group of children, and the rest all line up behind him. The procession moves around and the leader performs various actions; all the other children behind have to mimic those actions, and anyone that doesn't is out of the game. The last child left (other than the leader) wins, and becomes the new leader for the next round.

At Meadvale, a version known as 'Holy Gabriel' was played, having been invented by the Primitive Methodist School. It is reported that the game was completely unknown in any of the surrounding towns and villages, with the exception of the small village of Outwood, near Horley, where it was apparently introduced to the children by a stonemason who learned of the game from a cousin who had returned from America. The Meadvale version had its own rhyme that the children sang:

> Holy Gabriel, holy man,
> Rantum roarum reeden man,
> I'll do all as ever I can,
> To follow my Gabriel, holy man.

Former Primitive Methodist Chapel, Meadvale. (The Voice of Hassocks)

A Royal Secret

In April 1987, a national newspaper blew open a scandalous story that caused a sensation around the world. Officially, Nerissa and Katherine Bowes-Lyon – first-cousins to Elizabeth II – had been dead since 1940, but in reality they had been secretly sent to Royal Earlswood Asylum in 1941. The two girls had been born with learning disabilities, and were hidden away from the world for fear that their condition would bring scandal to the royal family and would impact upon the family's social standing.

The two girls were kept at Royal Earlswood in secrecy, although their mother, sister-in-law of the late Queen Mother, continued to visit them until her death in 1966. Additional shock was caused when it was revealed that the older sister, Nerissa, died the year before the news came out, and that she had been buried near the asylum in a grave marked only with a small plastic marker bearing the inscription 'M11125 Bowes-Lyon'. The story, it seems, had also been kept secret from several members of the Bowes-Lyon family.

It was also revealed that at the same time as the two cousins of the Queen were sent to the asylum, three other young members of the family (more distantly related) had also been admitted to Royal Earlswood at the same time. Katherine Bowes-Lyon remained living at the asylum until it closed down in 1997 following allegations of abuse, and was moved to another home in Surrey, where she died in 2014.

The story of the sisters was featured in an episode of *The Crown* in November 2020, which dramatised the shock of Princess Margaret learning about their existence.

The former Royal Earlswood Asylum. (RHaworth)

Murder in the Tunnel

The Merstham Tunnel (actually a pair of adjacent tunnels) was one of the first railway tunnels to be built in the UK and was officially opened in 1841, three years after work began on it. Considering they stretch for about a mile they are an impressive feat of early Victorian engineering. However, it was an event in 1905 that brought the tunnel its infamy.

Railways were attractive to those with nefarious motivations, and it's not particularly surprising that the long, dark Merstham Tunnel would become embroiled in criminal activity at some point.

That time came on 24 September 1905, when the mutilated body of Mary Money was found in the tunnel by a gang of railway workmen, and strange marks on the wall suggested that she hadn't simply been pushed (or jumped) out of a train. She also had a white silk scarf inserted down her throat, as well as being covered in scratches and bruises.

Mary had finished working in London at 7 p.m., purchased some chocolate in a nearby shop and informed a friend that she was going out for a walk. Instead, Mary headed to Victoria Station and boarded a train. Two guardsman – one at Purley and the other at East Croydon – both later reported having seen a couple on the train fighting, and the police supposed that Mary had met up with a secret lover and that it was he that murdered her. Mary was known to have dated a railway clerk, but he was able to provide an alibi as to his whereabouts at the time of Mary's death.

Extensive investigations could not find any culprit. In February 1906, a man handed himself into the police and confessed that he was the murderer, but he was dismissed as having suffered from 'delusions' and was instead admitted to an asylum. No one was ever charged or convicted for Mary's murder, and the case still remains unsolved to this day.

Merstham Tunnel, scene of an unsolved murder. (Peter Trimming)

The Merstham Wizard

Merstham has had some noteworthy rectors over the years, perhaps none more so than James Samborne, rector from 18 October 1679 until his death in February 1734. Unusual for a vicar, and especially in the sensitive years not long after the English Civil Wars, Revd Samborne was said to possess supernatural – perhaps even 'dark' – powers. The story told is that a thief was caught in the act by the reverend and attempted to escape by climbing a pear tree in the rectory garden. With the thief trapped, Revd Samborne (stood a safe distance away) fixed his gaze upon the man and using his special powers caused him to become stuck fast in the tree.

St Katherine's Church, Merstham. (Bill Boaden)

The Thornton Heath Vampire

The UK actually has quite a long, extensive history of vampire sightings dating back to the revenant burials of the Saxon era. Among the strangest of these cases occurred in an ordinary residential street in Thornton Heath.

This location is no stranger to paranormal events. In 1938 Alma Fielding, who lived with her family at No. 98 Beverstone Road, began to report strange activity at her home, including items being thrown through the air, or being able to summon up small animals out of thin air. The case was thoroughly investigated by psychical researchers, although opinions were split as to the cause of these events. The major theory was that Alma was exhibiting the phenomena through her own subconscious as a result of a repressed childhood trauma.

Although The Fielding case appears to have settled down, Thornton Heath was once again the centre of a supposed unnatural haunting in the early 1970s. Between 1972 and 1974, the Forbes family was plagued by similar violent manifestations, only this time it seems to have affected the entire family. The events began at Christmas in 1972, when decorations began to fly through the air with tremendous force. As time went on other things began to stir, and members of the family reported seeing ghosts or hearing mysterious noises. More unusual was that, on three separate occasions, Mrs Forbes claimed to have been attacked by a winged vampire that swooped down on her and bit her neck, leaving burn marks. She also claimed once to have been attacked by a phantom tiger, which left claw marks scratched across her arm. The house was blessed by a priest, but the events did not stop. Eventually, the family had to move out and stories of the vampire also appear to have fizzled out after this.

Seven Churches

Bletchingley has many points of interest, but it used to also be a village of great importance in the area. At one time it was its own borough, and was also retained as a separate parliamentary constituency until 1832, returning two Members of Parliament despite having an electorate of only about ten people. The village also sported a castle until 1264, and Bletchingley Place was the house to which Anne of Cleves retired after divorcing Henry VIII.

Tradition asserts that Bletchingley was so important in times past that it once had no less than seven churches. Local historian Granville Leveson-Gower supported this claim in the following way: St Mary the Virgin's Church at Horne was originally built as a chapel of ease to Bletchingley; the castle 'probably' had its own chapel; there were separate chapels at Ham and Daferons; an oratory at Stangrave; and 'if we suppose that the Old Manor House had a chapel', that would make up six churches, and St Mary's Church in the village would make the full seven.

If you thought that seven churches for one small village is a little excessive, then another legend asserts that Effingham once had sixteen.

Bletchingley Church, one of seven in the village – so we are told. (Gareth Williams)

Polly Paine

Polly Paine was the legendary village witch of Godstone who was able to transform herself into a hare. It appears that Polly was a good witch, for there are no stories about her performing evil deeds, and she appears to have got on well with the villagers despite their suspicions of her true identity. However, one day, when she had turned herself into a hare, she was chased by a pack of hunting hounds and received a deep laceration on her rear leg. The animal was seen to be chased into Polly's cottage in the woods. The next day Polly had to go into the village, but she had a bad limp and was unable to sit down properly, confirming in the minds of many that Polly was indeed a witch.

The story of Polly Paine still lives on at the village pub. (Stephen McKay)

John Trenchman

In a very prominent position in the churchyard at Godstone is a large headstone engraved with a skull and crossbones. Although associated with pirates, this symbol is actually quite a common one, although in the case of John Edward Trenchman, it inspired a legend.

The story goes that Trenchman became a mariner at a very early age and became embroiled in piracy in the Caribbean in the late seventeenth century, before returning home and becoming a smuggler instead, running contraband up from the coast and into northern Surrey.

All was well until one day a member of Trenchman's gang was caught, and in return for being spared his life, he spilled the beans on the local smuggling operation. With the excisemen now in full knowledge of the date and location of the next consignment of illicit goods, it was simply a matter of catching the smugglers in the act.

At Tilburstow Hill, near Godstone, the excisemen stood in wait, and as soon as Trenchman and his gang appeared they immediately came under musket fire. Trenchman was the only one to make his escape into the woods, although having been mortally wounded; he managed to hobble to the Fox and Hounds Inn, where he bled to death. Apparently, the villagers showed great sympathy and clubbed together to bury him in the local churchyard in an unmarked (and unconsecrated) grave.

However, Trenchman's spirit was not pleased with the treatment of his earthly remains. His ghost was said to regularly haunt and terrorise the graveyard, attacking gravediggers and leaving mysterious patches of blood in the church. A headstone was erected in the hope of appeasing the vengeful spirit, but it was fruitless, because the next day it was found smashed to pieces. Another headstone was erected, but that, too, was smashed, as was a third. It was not until the body of John Trenchman was exhumed and reburied with full rites closer to the church, and a headstone engraved with the skull and crossbones of a pirate erected, that Trenchman's spirit was finally laid to rest.

Grave of the supposed Godstone Pirate. (Dr Neil Clifton)

Lingfield Lock-up

In the very centre of Lingfield, standing beside the delightful little pond, is a curious small stone building that almost looks like it could be a miniature church. On the south-east side of this structure is a tower with a few small windows facing out; one of these has been blocked up with a plaque informing us that 'This Cross was built *circa* 1473 to designate the boundaries of Puttenden and Billeshurst Manors'. On the opposite side of the building, which can be reached in little more than a few strides, is a heavy wooden door inset with an iron grille and a pair of sturdy locks. This part of the building, the inscription tells us, is 'The Cage for the detention of petty offenders added in 1773 [and] was last used in 1882 to detain poachers'.

Another item of local interest stands adjacent to the lock-up. It is a large oak tree with a number of cavities around the base big enough to enter them. Once inside, the entire tree is completely hollow and large enough to allow a full-grown adult to stand upright inside and still have room to move about.

The Lingfield 'cage'. (Poliphilo)

The Crowhurst Yew

A tree so spectacular that Queen Victoria and Prince Albert are said to have made a special trip out from Windsor Castle to view it stands majestically in the grounds of St George's Church at Crowhurst. Thought by some to be 4,000 years old and others stating 'just' 1,500 years old, it certainly has a varied history.

The tree is first recorded in 1630, when it was already 30 feet in circumference, and since when it has added a further 4 feet to its girth. As is the case with many great yews, the interior has been hollowed out, leaving a sizeable chasm in the centre. At some point by the early eighteenth century a wooden door had been installed into the side of the trunk (which still survives), giving access into the 'room' inside – large enough to accommodate about a dozen people. In fact, this room used to house a table and chairs, and it is said that the local council used it as their meeting place, and that it was also once the home of a family who lost their house.

Unfortunately, this fine specimen has also suffered other ravages of time. A Civil War era cannonball was once found embedded within its wood, and in the early 1920s various pieces of scrap metal – tea trays, kettles, pan lids – had been nailed to the trunk and painted bright red; these 'patches' were supposedly done to repair other damage to the tree.

Other large yew trees in Surrey have their own folklore associated with them. The one in St Peter's churchyard at Hambledon is said to house a witch who will appear if you circle around the hollow interior three times. Similarly, at Capel a ghost is meant to appear to anyone who manages to walk around the yew tree 100 times at the stroke of midnight.

The Crowhurst Yew.
(Donald Macauley)

Left: The wooden door in the Crowhurst Yew. (Peter Trimming)

Below: The Hambledon Yew. (Dave Spicer)

A Busy Man

The rhyme immortalising Henry VIII's six wives is still as popular as ever, but at Crowhurst there was another Tudor nobleman who gave the king a run for his money.

The Gainsford family held Crowhurst Place from 1338 and appear to have maintained a tradition of naming the oldest son John. After seven generations of Johns came Sir John Gainsford, born around 1469. He served at least two terms as Sheriff of Surrey in 1501 and 1518, and he was also a member of Henry VIII's inner circle.

None of this, however, seemed to have kept Sir John particularly busy, because he also had six wives. The first five wives brought him no fewer than fifteen daughters, and it wasn't until his sixth and final wife that Sir John got the son and heir he so desired – a total of sixteen children!

Crowhurst Place, former seat of Sir John Gainsford. (Kurseong Carl)

Moll Cutpurse

We've seen in a previous chapter that Surrey had its share of highwaymen, but what about highwaywomen? The 'profession' wasn't limited to men only, and Surrey allegedly had its own female villain by the name of Mary Frith, better known as Moll Cutpurse. As is the case with all such stories, Mary's life has been greatly exaggerated and mythologised over the years. She was born in London in the 1580s and was a notorious thief and pickpocket around the city, hence her nickname (Moll = a disreputable woman, Cutpurse = pickpocket), and was regularly in trouble with the law. In her twenties, Mary began to dress in men's clothing and perform in pubs and taverns across London, gaining an infamous reputation for bawdy living and 'unwomanly' activities. Some of her performances landed her in gaol on various charges. In later life she became involved in prostitution, but it is one (almost certainly false) legend that has landed her a place in Surrey folklore. While living her life in London, Mary was said to also be a highwaywoman in the northern parts of Surrey, and was quite successful by all accounts. Her most daring act was holding up the coach of Sir Thomas Fairfax, the commander of the Parliamentarian army in the English Civil War, in 1651, robbing him of £250 (and in some stories shooting Fairfax in the arm). She made her escape, but Fairfax was relentless in his pursuit and eventually caught her. She was sent to Newgate Prison and was due to be sent to the gallows, but purchased her freedom with a fine of £2,000.

Moll Cutpurse. (Wellcome Collection)

Gambling Disc

In many Surrey pubs in the early to mid-Victorian era, a black wooden disk could be found nailed to the underside of a ceiling beam near the fireplace. On it would have been the numbers 1 to 12 painted in white so that it resembled a clock face. In the centre an iron pointer was attached on a pivot so that when flicked it would spin freely, and three men would take turns spinning it with either their hands or a stick. The man who got the highest total score from three spins was the winner and would drink free at his friends' expense that night. Towards the end of the century, the game was frowned upon as a form of gambling and the discs were removed.

A Gambling Disc in a Surrey pub. (*Old West Surrey*)

Snail Charming

An old favourite pastime for Surrey children was the game of snail charming. When a snail was found the children would try and charm it out of its shell by repeating the rhyme 'Snail, snail, come out of your hole; Or else I'll beat you as black as coal' over and over until it had the desired effect and the snail appeared. Apparently this gave much amusement to the children.

A 'charming' Surrey snail. (Peter Trimming)

Weather Lore

The weather is an important and common aspect in folklore, and Surrey can boast several such tales of foretelling the weather. For example, if the weather on Candlemas Day (2 February) is dry and sunny, then the snow will blow in again before May. If, however, Candlemas Day is cold and wet, the winter is gone and will not come again; whatever the weather is on Kingston Fair day (13 November) will predominate for the rest of the season. Godalming Fair Day fell precisely three months after Kingston's and if the sun shone before noon on that day, then winter would last another three months. If Christmas Day falls on a new moon, then the wheat harvest in the coming year will be plentiful. Conversely, however, if the new moon falls on any Saturday in the year, then it is a bad omen for the weather to come and usually foretold of rain or destructive storms on their way. We are also informed that in Surrey 'it's always cold when the blackthorn comes into flower'. Local pig farmers were also said to believe that the animals could see the wind, and this is why they became restless in such weather.

Folk-Medicine

Folk-remedies for various ailments were also once popular, particularly in days when healthcare was expensive or non-existent. In Surrey it was advised that parsley should not be grown in the garden otherwise a death will occur before the year is out. In many parts of the UK, stroking the fingers of a freshly executed criminal across the neck of a young girl or woman was said to cure several ailments, and in Surrey it was the custom to mark the sign of the cross on the neck with the dead convict's hand as a certain cure for goitre. The shingles could be cured by scraping off the corrosion (known as the 'comb') from a church bell and rub it onto the inflicted. Meanwhile, whooping cough could be kept at bay by preserving a cross-bun from one Good Friday to the next (in fact, any foodstuffs baked on Good Friday were said to keep for as long as twelve years and still be edible). Similarly, rain water caught on Holy Thursday and stored in a corked bottle will never stagnate. Carrying a knucklebone on your person would cure rheumatism, while tying a small bag around a baby's neck containing one of the mother's lost teeth was meant to help stop teething pains. A mole's foot kept in one's pocket kept cramp at bay – but it had to be one of the poor mole's front feet to work. Reigate was also blessed with its own wise woman in 1851 when a healer made her appearance near the town; she would give someone afflicted with a minor ailment a rhyme to recite. A woman scalded by boiling water went to the women, and upon reciting the poem was fully healed within the week. A long (and seemingly unnatural life) could be had by sleeping on a game-feather mattress. When ailing or elderly individuals were ready to 'pass on', they were moved to a different bed otherwise their spirit would not be allowed to leave their bodies. At the opposite end of the lifecycle, a baby suffering from fits could be given a drop of sacramental wine in some parts of Surrey to cure the condition.

Bells at St John the Evangelist's Church, Churt. (Hassocks5489)

Surrey Puma

Since the 1950s, dozens of sightings of the infamous Surrey Puma have been reported – the Godalming area alone is said to have registered 362 sightings in the two years from September 1964.

The first reports came from Farnham in 1959, and over the next several years the sightings of the mysterious creature came in from a wider area, including adjoining parts of Hampshire and south-east London. In 1964, a plaster cast of a paw print was handed into Godalming police station, which, when compared to a specimen held at London Zoo, was identified as being that of a puma.

Sightings tailed off towards the end of the decade, with just a few isolated and unconfirmed reports being made. In 1975 a boy at Chiddingfold reported a large cat-like animal in some nearby woods, and in 1984 some hairs were found at Peaslake that were found to be puma fur during testing. The last sighting of the twentieth century occurred in 1995 when a serving police officer claimed to have seen the puma outside a school in Effingham.

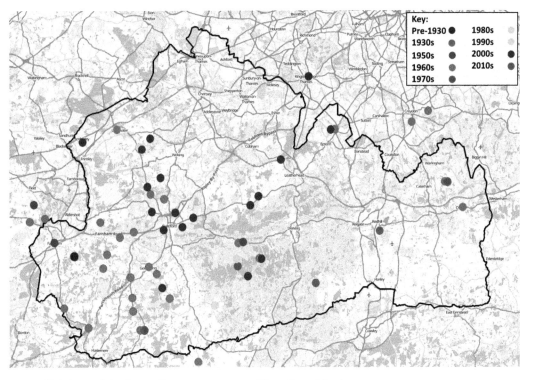

Sightings of the Surrey Puma 1770–2019. (OpenStreetMap)

The case went cold for several years, but a new wave of sightings began in 2003, when a high-ranking police officer reported seeing the animal at Holmbury Hill. The following year, several residents of Abinger Common saw a large cat in local woods and farmland. Then, in 2005 the creature was finally captured on film showing a large brown-coloured cat about the size of a large dog, which was identified by experts as a lynx. Other images came in during the year and seemed to indicate that there were two species living in Surrey – the lynx and another that resembled a puma. Many of the reports have been dismissed by various experts, who state that it would not be possible for such animals to live in numbers required to breed in Surrey. Throughout the rest of the decade, scattered sightings were reported to the media from as far apart as Camberley and Chobham in the north-west to Newdigate in the south-east. The most recent suspected sighting, at the time of writing, was of a large cat-like animal on the outskirts of Redhill in 2019, followed a couple of days later by the discovery of a mutilated deer carcass nearby.

Despite all this, the phenomenon is not a modern one. William Cobbett wrote of having seen a large cat at Waverley Abbey in 1770, and several sightings of such creatures were reported across Surrey in the 1930s.

Image Credits

Public Domain – Hassocks5489: St John the Evangelist's Church, Old Kiln Lane, Churt (June 2015) (Bell-cot); St Margaret's Church, Coles Lane, Ockley (July 2013) (Churchyard). The Voice of Hassocks: Former Primitive Methodist Chapel, Lower Road, Meadvale (June 2013). Poliphilo: Cross and Cage, Lingfield. Jack1956: Holy Trinity Church Guildford Abbot Tomb Above; William Cobbett Grave 2016. Immanuel Giel: Park Reigate. SuzanneKn: Anchoress of Shere. *A Handbook of Dorking*, p. 28. *Old West Surrey*, p. 246.

CC-BY-SA 2.0 (https://creativecommons.org/licenses/by-sa/2.0/) – ©Kurseong Carl: Crowhurst Place. ©David Howard: Exit to Potters Lane on the A3; View across the North Downs, Betchworth. ©Banalities: Newlands Corner. ©Stefan Czapski: Level-crossing and station buildings, Chilworth; The Watts Cemetery Chapel, Compton. ©Lewis Clarke: Surrey: Mole Valley – Okley [*sic*] from the Air. ©Gareth Williams: Bletchingley Church – Sept 2010 – Exterior. ©N. Chadwick: Shag Brook; Wagamama. ©Alan Hunt: Bullbeggars Lane; The Jolly Farmer roundabout; Silent Pool, Albury; St Ann's Hill; Frieze, Watts mortuary chapel. ©Len Williams: The Obelisk, Camberley; War of the Worlds. ©Don Cload: Trees by the North Downs Way; Chobham Common. ©Donald Macauley: The Crowhurst Yew. ©Dave Spicer: Yew tree in St Peter's graveyard. ©Peter Trimming: The Crowhurst Yew, Crowhurst, Surrey; Tunnel at Merstham; Stone Circle, West Byfleet; 'Brian' the Snail. ©Mike Pennington: Path in woodland at Nonsuch Park. ©Alan Simkins: Lingfield Old Gaol. ©Ian Capper: Fetcham Mill Pond; Wray Common Road railway bridge; Rose-ringed Parakeet (*Psittacula krameri*); Entrance to the Swan Chopping Centre; St Martin's Church. ©Andrew Bowden: Mother Ludlam's Cave. ©Andrew West: Father Foote's Cave. ©Dave Kelly: Ockley, St Margaret. ©Dr Neil Clifton: Godstone, Surrey: Gravestone with skull and bones. ©Stephen McKay: Pub sign and bus stop, Godstone. ©Bill Nicholls: A piece of track; Across the Refectory. ©Mark Percy: Former necropolis railway platform; St Catherine's Chapel; St Martha's Church. ©Dominic Alves: Barons' Sand Caves and Mine, Reigate. ©Colin Smith: Through the Open Window; West Horsley Place; George Abbott; George Abbott; Historic Cottages, Great Bookham; Chobham Cannon; Heathland, Horsell Common; West Clandon Serpent; Sundial, West Clandon; Parkside School. ©John Salmon: St Nicholas, Cranleigh; St Nicholas, Cranleigh – Churchyard; St Mary West Horsley – Wall monument. ©Bill Boaden: St Katharine's Church, Merstham. ©Nick Richards: Woking 'art'; Woking Martian Caption. ©Julian Osley: "William Cobbett public house. ©James Emmans: The Fox Way on Cobbett Hill. ©Allen Watkin:

Bibliography

Aubrey, John, *The Natural History and Antiquities of Surrey* Vol. 3 (London: E. Curll, 1718).

Brayley, Edward Wedlake, *A Topographical History of Surrey* Vol. 2 (London: G. Willis, 1850).

Brayley, Edward Wedlake, *Choice Notes From Notes and Queries: Folklore* (London: Bell and Daldy, 1859).

Clinch, George, and Kershaw, S. W. (eds.), *Bygone Surrey* (London: Simpkin, Marshall, Hamilton, Kent & Co., 1895).

Cobbett, William, *Cobbett's Political Register* Vol. 11 (London: Cox and Baylis, 1807).

Collyer, Graham, *The Surrey Village Book* (Newbury: Countryside Books, 1990 [1984]).

Cox, J. Charles (ed.), *Memorials of Old Surrey* (London: George Allen & Sons, 1911).

Dashwood, J. B., *The Thames to the Solent* (London: Longmans, Green & Co., 1868).

Dugdale, Thomas, and Burnett, William, *Curiosities of Great Britain* Vol. 1 (1835).

Dyer, T. F. Thiselton, *Strange Pages from Family Papers* (London: Sampson Low, Marston and Co, 1895).

Folkard, Richard, *Plant Lore, Legends, and Lyrics* (London: Sampson Low, Marston, Searle, and Rivington, 1884).

The Folk-Lore Society, *Publications of the Folk-Lore Society* Vol. 4 (London: W. Satchell, Peyton and Co, 1881).

The Folk-Lore Society, *Publications of the Folk-Lore Society* Vol. 35 (London: David Nutt, 1895).

Gomme, George Laurence (ed.), *The Gentleman's Magazine Library: Manners and Customs* (London: Elliot Stock, 1883).

Gomme, George Laurence (ed.), *The Gentleman's Magazine Library: Popular Superstitions* Vol. 3 (London: Elliott Stock, 1884).

Gomme, George Laurence (ed.), *A Dictionary of British Folk-Lore* Vol. 1 (London: David Nutt, 1894).

Harper, Charles G., *Haunted Houses* (London: Chapman & Hall, 1907).

Jekyll, Gertrude, *Old West Surrey* (London: Longmans, Green & Co., 1904).

Jerrold, Walter, *Surrey* (London: J. M. Dent, 1901).

Johnson, Charles, *The History of the Lives and Actions of the Most Famous Highwaymen* (Edinburgh: John Thompson Jr & Co., 1814).

L'Estrange Ewen, C., *Witch Hunting and Witch Trials* (New York: The Dial Press, 1929).

Lovett, Edward, *Folk-Lore & Legend of the Surrey Hills and of the Sussex Downs & Forests* (Caterham: 1928).

Lysons, Daniel, *The Environs of London* Vol. 1 (London: T. Cadell and W. Davies, 1792).

Mackinlay, James M., *Folklore of Scottish Lochs and Springs* (Glasgow: William Hodge & Co., 1893).

Northall, G. F., *English Folk-Rhymes* (London: Kegan, Paul, Trench, Trübner & Co., 1892).

Parker, Eric, *Highways and Byways in Surrey* (London: Macmillan, 1921).

Sharpe, J. A., *Dick Turpin: The Myth of the English Highwayman* (London: Profile Books, 2005 [2004]).

Soane, George, *Curiosities of Literature* Vol. 1 (London: E. Churton, 1847).

Strange and Wonderful News from Yowel in Surry, &c (London: J. Clarke, 1681).

Surrey Archaeological Society, *Collections of the Surrey Archaeological Society* Vol.5 Part 2 (London: Wyman & Sons, 1871).

Thompson, Denys, *Change and Tradition in Rural England* (Cambridge: Cambridge University Press, 1980).

Turner, M. C., *A Saunter Through Surrey* (London: W. Walker, 1857).

Vaux, Rev. J. Edward, *Church Folklore* (London: Griffith Farran & Co., 1894).

Wickham Legg, Leopold G. (ed.), *English Coronation Records* (Westminster: Archibald Constable & Co., 1901).

Woodhouse, Reginald Illingworth, and Pearman, A. J., Fisher, Thomas, *The Registers of Merstham, Surrey 1538–1812* (London: The Parish Register Society, 1902).

The *Cambrian*, 9 February 1906.

The *Gentleman's Magazine*, October 1796.

The *Gentleman's Magazine*, July 1800.

The *Gentleman's Magazine*, December 1827.

The *Gentleman's Magazine*, Vol. 259, 1885.

The *Gentleman's Magazine*, Vol. 262, 1887.

The *Gentleman's Magazine*, Vol. 267, 1889.

Notes and Queries Series 1, Vol. 4, 18 October 1851.

Notes and Queries Series 5, Vol. 10, 13 July, 14 September, 15 December 1878.

Notes and Queries Series 6, Vol. 5, 11, 25 February, 6 May 1882.

Notes and Queries Series 6, Vol. 6, 15 July, 19 August 1882.

Notes and Queries Series 7, Vol. 2, London, 1886.

Weekly Journal, 19 November 1726.

Agatha and Poirot: Partners in Crime, (2021). [TV Programme] ITV: 5 April 2021.

Great British Railway Journeys, S. 12 Ep. 4 'Guildford to Aldershot' (2021). [TV Programme] BBC2: 29 April 2021.

Tony Robinson's History of Britain, S. 1 Ep. 1 'The Tudors' (2020). [TV Programme] Channel 5: 4 January 2020.